ANF

Items should be returned to any Gloucestershire County Library on or
before the date stamped below. This book remains the property of the
Brockworth Community Library and can be renewed in person or by
telephone by calling 01452 862 730

07/21   635

17/6/21

4/11/21

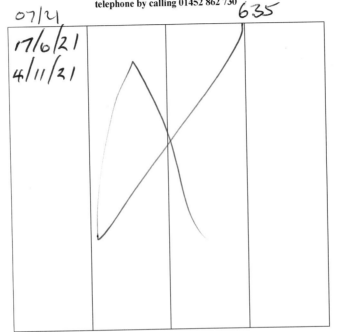

garden
WISDOM

Jenny Hendy

garden
WISDOM

Gardening hints & tips from yesteryear

LORENZ BOOKS

This edition is published by Lorenz Books

Lorenz Books is an imprint of
Anness Publishing Ltd
Hermes House
88–89 Blackfriars Road
London SE1 8HA
tel. 020 7401 2077; fax 020 7633 9499
www.lorenzbooks.com; info@anness.com

© Anness Publishing Ltd 2003

UK agent: The Manning Partnership Ltd, 6 The Old
Dairy, Melcombe Road, Bath BA2 3LR; tel. 01225
478 444; fax 01225 478 440; sales@manning-
partnership.co.uk

UK distributor: Grantham Book Services Ltd
Isaac Newton Way
Alma Park Industrial Estate
Grantham
Lincs NG31 9SD;
tel. 01476 541080; fax 01476 541061
orders@gbs.tbs-ltd.co.uk

North American agent/distributor:
National Book Network
4501 Forbes Boulevard
Suite 200
Lanham, MD 20706
tel. 301 459 3366; fax 301 429 5746
www.nbnbooks.com

Australian agent/distributor:
Pan Macmillan Australia
Level 18, St Martins Tower
31 Market St
Sydney, NSW 2000
tel. 1300 135 113; fax 1300 135 103
customer.service@macmillan.com.au

A CIP catalogue record for this book is available
from the British Library.

PUBLISHER: Joanna Lorenz
MANAGING EDITOR: Helen Sudell
PROJECT EDITOR: Simona Hill
DESIGNER: Louise Clements
EDITORIAL READER: Penelope Goodare
PRODUCTION CONTROLLER: Darren Price

10 9 8 7 6 5 4 3 2 1

Contents

Introduction

Many of the gardening techniques and practices of the past were born out of a deep understanding of nature. Back then people living in the country had a more intimate relationship with the land they depended on. Today, we spend large amounts of time living and working in artificial environments, where we are cut off from the natural rhythms of the seasons. Our pace of life is so frenetic that we simply don't take the time, as the saying goes, to smell the roses. Now, however, an increasing number of people are questioning such lifestyles. Our need to establish a grounding connection with the earth is primal, and one of the most natural and satisfying ways to slow down the pace of life is by working the land in our own gardens.

It's been said that there's nothing new in gardening. After centuries of trial and error, certain techniques have been perfected, and even with today's sophisticated technology we can do little to improve them. If you compare the way people gardened in history with the approach of modern organic gardeners, there are many similarities. Gardening has, in fact, come full circle. The wisdom of caring for the soil and of finding ways to work in harmony with nature is being rediscovered by a new generation of gardeners.

One factor that shaped the way that gardening was carried out in the past was that tools and materials had to last. Our forebears did not live in a throwaway society; it was necessary to make do and mend. A perfect example is the clay pot. In the days of Victorian country estates, a head gardener couldn't simply pop down to the local garden centre to pick up a replacement batch. The pots came in a wide variety of shapes and sizes. Some were plain, and others were highly ornate, but each one had a specific use. This collection would be recycled repeatedly, and one of the arduous tasks of the under-gardeners was to scrub the pots clean. Another task was to soak new terracotta before use, as ultra-dry clay would extract moisture from the compost. If large pots developed cracks but weren't too badly damaged, they were held together with galvanized wire – an elegant craft that has largely died out today. Any broken pieces of pot were, of course, collected for 'crocking' (breaking up and using as drainage material in a pot), or to provide extra drainage for moisture-sensitive plants. Knowledge was passed down from gardener to apprentice, but many of the tricks of the trade were lost when men went off to fight in World War I, or found more lucrative employment in manufacturing.

Clay pots were made to be reused and the care exercised by the gardeners of yesteryear means that antique pots are still available.

On the surface, the modern trends of 'instant' and low-maintenance gardening seem quite appealing, but one of the benefits of carrying out traditional garden tasks by hand is that, quite apart from the end result, the actual process is so satisfying. When occupied with the business of gardening – weeding, dead-heading, pruning, mowing, sowing, potting up, sweeping and raking – the day feels as though it is passing by more slowly. There's also much to be said for setting aside the time to care for gardening tools and equipment, and for taking pride in a neat and well-organized potting shed.

Gardeners have always striven to improve on nature. Over the centuries, plant varieties have been selected for a host of characteristics, and some plants have changed immeasurably. Gardens today are full of fruits, vegetables and flowers from around the globe. We've undoubtedly benefited from disease-resistant strains, and from plants that flower more freely or crop more heavily, but many of the old varieties and plants that are relatively close to their wild ancestry also perform well and manifest fewer problems than the exotics that fill our plots.

That is not to say that all of the old ways are better. No one today, for example, would want to use nicotine sprays for fruit trees, and it would be impractical and anti-social for a small town garden to house a manure heap! There are times when we appreciate modern machinery, and we now have all kinds of new materials at our disposal, including horticultural fleece and landscaping fabric. Here the best of both worlds are brought together to show how you can marry old and new to benefit both your plot and your sense of wellbeing.

Top right: This tiny garden shed is a relic from the past, with its age-worn timbers and tiled roof. As well as having practical use, a building like this can make an attractive focus for the garden.
Right: Old-fashioned sweet peas have a rich fragrance and soft colouring, and any variety has cottage garden appeal.

Flower Garden

What is a garden without flowers? These fragile,

ephemeral, many-coloured jewels transform our

outdoor world. Each day brings new delights, from

the dew-spangled petals of early morning

to the sun-worshipping blooms of midday

and the intoxicating perfumes of twilight.

The fragile beauty and fragrance of flowers affect us on an emotional level and even non-gardeners admit to being passionate about a particular bloom or flower colour. Certain kinds of flower also help to create a style or look for the garden. For example blooms with a bold sculptural form can appear contemporary or sub-tropical, while those with sumptuous frills and flounces are unquestionably romantic. Many people fear that the herbaceous perennials, biennials, bulbs and annuals of a traditional flower border involve far more work than their busy schedules permit. It's true that the herbaceous borders of old required quite a lot of maintenance to keep them in peak condition. Seasonal tasks involved lifting and dividing crowns to maintain vigour; bedding out tender plants; staking tall or unruly varieties, as well as feeding, mulching, watering and deadheading. Fortunately nowadays there are scores of perennials that require very little attention.

Hellebores and delicate windflowers make an easy-care combination for dappled shady areas.

For those who love flowers but don't have time to look after a traditional herbaceous border, mixed borders with long-flowering shrubs and roses, mingled with low-maintenance perennials, are an excellent solution.

Before the advent of garden centres, gardeners bought some young plants from their local greengrocer, garden or hardware store, but most plants were grown by gardeners from seed (saving their own whenever possible), or from cuttings shared among neighbours. Large numbers of plants can be raised for relatively little outlay, and the old-fashioned species and varieties still stocked by seedsmen often have more scent and charm than their modern counterparts. It is immensely rewarding to grow plants from seed, and hardy annuals could not be easier. With their vibrant blooms, they make great gap fillers.

Honeysuckle and roses weave an informal archway to the garden beyond.

Well-tended lawns are a perfect foil for beautiful foliage and flowers.

Use English roses for their period looks and improved disease resistance.

Pink cow parsley has the look of a wild flower with ferny foliage.

Though hardy annuals can be simply sown where they are to flower, many seeds are difficult to grow without a greenhouse or propagator. For those who don't have these facilities, buying plants from the garden centre is the answer. Many of us also don't have space for a dedicated seed bed, where biennials can be raised the year before they flower, but fortunately the range of old-fashioned cottage flowers on offer includes forget-me-nots, wallflowers, double daisies, pansies, foxgloves, sweet Williams, stocks and hollyhocks, all ready to plant out from autumn through to spring. However, a few plants have slipped through the net. Honesty (*Lunaria annua*), whose medieval names of lunary and moonwort referred to the silvery moon-like seed heads, as well as dame's violet or sweet rocket (*Hesperis matronalis*), a simple flower with an intoxicating twilight fragrance, rarely make an appearance as young plants, but are easily grown from seed. Like granny's bonnets (*Aquilegia*), sweet rocket is a short-lived perennial best treated as an annual or a biennial. Once introduced into your garden, however, this and many other old-fashioned flowers such as forget-me-not and sweet William will self-seed and bloom again year after year. Bear in mind that the modern technique of mulching may prevent this natural regeneration.

Cottage Borders

The seemingly carefree style of the traditional cottage garden was originally born out of necessity rather than the desire for an aesthetically pleasing garden.

COTTAGE DWELLERS DEPENDED on their gardens to supplement their diet and to provide them with many of the materials necessary for daily life. Every plant had to earn its place and most had more than one use. As well as keeping livestock, the household grew food plants, herbs and flowers, which were all mixed together in the same small area. This method of gardening makes a great deal of sense practically, as pests are confused by the jumbled signals they receive, and are less able to home in on a particular target.

Some varieties of flower and herb were grown to eat; others were used for flavouring and preserving food, dyeing textiles, and for medical purposes, as well as to keep moths at bay. Growing a range of flowers also helped ensure that there were plenty of beneficial insects, keeping pest numbers down.

LEFT: Sweet peas, in a range of soft pinks and purples, make a lovely decorative boundary to this vegetable garden. The old-fashioned mixtures have the best scent. Mice love the seeds; to deter them, try coating them with paraffin and sowing them with a covering of prickly leaves, or start plants under glass in early spring. Nick the hard seed coat on the opposite side to the 'eye' to help the seed to absorb moisture, and plant in tubes made from rolled newspaper. These allow you to plant

ABOVE: Many ornamental, old-fashioned flowers have survived because of their past medicinal or culinary use.

the seedlings out 'pot' and all, avoiding damage to the fragile taproot. Sweet peas will stop flowering if the soil is too dry, so make sure the ground is well manured. For strong bushy plants, pinch out seedlings when they have two pairs of leaves. Remember, the more flowers you pick, the more abundantly they will flower.

ABOVE: Some cottage blooms, such as opium poppies and the granny's bonnets (*Aquilegia*) shown here, self-seed readily and can be left from year to year. If they need a little more help, you can do as gardeners did in the past, and collect the ripe seeds for sowing. Not all flowers come true but many perennial varieties, including ornamental onions, Jacob's ladder (*Polemonium*) and *Geum* 'Mrs J Bradshaw' are well worth collecting. Wait until the seeds in a sample pod have turned black or brown – they will often rattle. Cut the stems and shake the heads into a paper bag to collect the seed.

Annuals from Seed

Most cottage annuals are easy to grow from seed and can be sown in situ, either broadcast, or in rows, for easier identification when weeding. Sow at two-week intervals from mid-spring until midsummer, to ensure a succession of blooms right through till autumn. Try love-in-a-mist (Nigella), pot marigold (Calendula), sweet candytuft (Iberis) and the mignonette (Reseda).

1 Working on a patch of moist, friable soil, rake the surface to a fine tilth.

2 Using a cane or dibber, mark out parallel rows for sowing one variety. Angle the rows in a different direction to sow an adjacent area.

3 Sow the seed of each variety as thinly as possible, keeping taller types towards the back. Lightly cover with soil by moving the back of the rake along the rows. Firm lightly.

FLOWERS FOR THE HOUSE

It's very satisfying to cut home-grown flowers for the house, but results can be disappointing unless you follow a few simple rules.

- Cut flowers in the cool of the evening and place the stems in water straight away.

- Cut stems of plants such as delphiniums and snapdragons just above a side shoot to encourage further flowering.

- Leave flowers standing up to their necks in water overnight, using tall, traditional flower buckets (a process known as conditioning). Trim stems to the required size and arrange.

- Gardening lore states that foxglove leaves help keep arrangements fresh for longer; you can simply add an infusion of their leaves to the water.

- Daffodils shouldn't be mixed with other blooms, but last well on their own with a lump of charcoal.

Roses – the Gift of Angels

The rose is one of the oldest plants in cultivation. Its fragrance is legendary and is one of the main reasons for its enduring popularity.

ALTHOUGH THE ROSE was revered by the ancient Greeks and Romans, the home of the rose garden is Persia. There, the rosaries so enchanted the conquering Moors that they took up the art of rose-growing and carried it to Europe. In medieval Britain, the rose became the flower of flowers, and *Rosa gallica*, the damask rose (*Rosa damascena*) and *Rosa* x *alba* were grown alongside the lily in religiously symbolic 'paradise gardens'. More practically, roses were also used for flavouring food and scenting linens, and as aromatherapists will confirm, the oil has strong healing powers.

The modern method of growing roses has not helped the plant's reputation as a difficult garden subject. Keeping large groups together in beds of bare soil, excluding all other plants, has encouraged

the spread of fungal diseases, and frequent spraying is usually recommended to control rust, blackspot and mildew, as well as the troublesome aphid. However, by following the companion planting approach, you could still include many of the delightful old roses, not noted for their disease resistance, such as 'Mme Isaac Pereire' and 'Cardinal de Richelieu'.

ABOVE & LEFT: Roses use up certain trace elements rapidly and can suffer from nutrient deficiencies. Regular manuring in winter helps to maintain fertility, and you can also use banana skins. Place them around the plants just under the soil level and they will rot down to release calcium, magnesium, phosphates, silica, sodium and sulphur.

Rose Companions

Mixing roses with 'protective' plants is one of the best ways to ensure their health. An appropriate underplanting can act just like a tonic and even help to revive an ailing collection. Many of the herbs detailed below have a long history of association with the rose, partly because of its ancient role within medicine. Parsley and garlic are said to increase the fragrance of roses, provided you don't allow the garlic to flower and release its own odour! Underplanting with tulips attracts mice, so use dwarf daffodils instead.

- Bergamot (bee balm) (*Monarda didyma*)
- Borage (*Borago officinalis*)
- Chives (*Allium schoenoprasum*) – aphid repellent, maintains health
- Crown imperial (*Fritillaria imperialis*)
- French marigold (*Tagetes patula*) – controls eelworm/nematode. Attracts the aphids' enemies – hoverflies
- Garlic (*Allium sativum*) – Aphid and mouse repellent. Maintains good health
- Hyssop (*Hyssopus officinalis*)
- Lavender (*Lavandula*) – ant repellent
- Lemon balm (*Melissa officinalis*)
- Lily species (e.g. *Lilium martagon*, *L. candidum*)
- Mallow family (e.g. *Malva moschata* 'Alba')
- Mullein (*Verbascum* spp.)
- Nasturtium (*Tropaeolum majus*) – discourages weeds and maintains health
- Ornamental allium – aphid repellent
- Parsley (*Petroselinum crispum*) – aphid repellent
- Poached egg plant (*Limnanthes douglasii*) – attracts hoverflies
- Pot marigold (*Calendula officinalis*) – controls eelworm/nematode. Attracts beneficial hoverflies
- Rosemary (*Rosmarinus officinalis* and cultivars) – ant repellant
- Rue (*Ruta graveolens*, e.g. 'Jackman's Blue') (can be a severe skin irritant)
- Sage (*Salvia officinalis*) – aphid repellent
- Thyme (*Thymus* spp.)
- Wild chamomile (*Matricaria recutita*)

ABOVE: There is a tendency for climbing roses to get a little threadbare at the base, and they may be out of flower for periods during the spring and summer. By growing other climbers with roses, you can often fill in the gaps and create some wonderful flowering combinations. Match the size and vigour of the climber to that of the rose, otherwise one will swamp the other. You also need to make sure that the pruning regime is compatible. Some possibilities are: clematis (large-flowered hybrids; viticella types; early-flowering *Clematis alpina* and *C. macropetala* cultivars), Chilean potato tree (*Solanum crispum* 'Glasnevin'), honeysuckle (*Lonicera periclymenum* 'Belgica' or 'Serotina'), jasmine (*Jasminum officinale* or *J.* x *stephanense*), potato vine (*Solanum laxum* 'Album') and star jasmine (*Trachelospermum jasminoides*).

A Verdant Backdrop

Grass has been used to create lawns since medieval times, but in those days the carefully tended 'flowery meads' were grown luxuriantly long and embroidered with sundry flowers, such as daisy, violet and periwinkle.

THE FLOWER MEADOWS of medieval times were 'fragrant carpets to be walked, danced, sat and lain upon' and today's lawn weeds were popular flowers, particularly the daisy. Its name comes from the Anglo-Saxon 'daezeseye', or 'eye of day', for its yellow sun-like centre and the fact that it closes up at night.

Nowadays lawns are chiefly used to create tranquil open spaces that act as a foil for border flowers. Some gardeners become vexed when a dandelion or buttercup pops up to mar the sward. For others a lawn just wouldn't be the same without carpets of daisies, clover, self-heal or the pretty, blue-flowered speedwell.

Moles can play havoc with your turf but, on the positive side, the soil collected from molehills is wonderfully friable and, when blended with sharp sand, makes the perfect potting mix! Perhaps the most common problem with lawns is moss. It colonizes when the turf is weak, especially when it is mown too close, or growing in shaded or poorly drained spots. The solution is to sort out the unfavourable growing conditions with good cultivation.

ABOVE: Rake lawns lightly once a month in summer, using a spring tine lawn rake, to prevent a build-up of dead grass, known as thatch. Alternatively, hire a scarifying machine to go over the lawn in late summer or early spring. To rejuvenate patches of poor quality turf, aerate by pushing a digging fork into the ground and rocking it forwards and backwards very slightly before moving to the next position, 10–15cm/4–6in away. Walk backwards to avoid compacting the soil.

When operating traditional lawn edging shears, to keep the action smooth and efficient, keep the handle attached to the bottom blade steady, and move the top blade handle in and out. Re-cut the lawn edge as necessary, using a sharp, half-moon iron.

ABOVE: Traditional weeding tools included the daisy grubber and, for stubborn, tap-rooted individuals, the curiously named spudding fork. These tools are highly effective for removing coarse weeds such as dandelion and plantain. You can also use a kitchen knife, screwdriver, or narrow trowel. Alternatively, to avoid a lawn full of holes, remove all the leaves at least once a week – the weeds will eventually weaken and die.

LEFT: The besom, a broom made from bundles of twigs, is very useful for lawn work. It can be used to disperse earthworm casts before mowing, particularly on sticky clay, so that the soil doesn't smear over the grass. Use it to brush in the annual, late-spring top-dressing of equal parts garden compost and sharp sand, and in autumn it's perfect for gathering up the leaves to lessen the risk of fungal disease.

TIPS FOR MOWING

The sweeping lawns of the great mansion houses were once cut with scythes and sometimes also hand shears if a really fine finish was required. It wasn't until the cylinder mower was invented in 1830 that grass cutting began to be less of a chore.

Even with recent high-tech advances, a cylinder mower is still the best option for a high-quality lawn, although for successful cutting, the blades need to be kept sharp and properly aligned. A rotary mower, with the option of a rear roller for producing stripes, is rather less demanding but still gives a good cut. To avoid classic problems, such as scalping and scorching in summer, follow these guidelines:

- Fill in hollows with a compost/sand mix and peel back the turf on hummocks to remove excess soil.
- Set the cutting height to around 2.5cm/1in for an everyday lawn. Close mowing encourages daisies and moss.
- Cut regularly when the grass is actively growing (once or twice a week in summer).
- Raise the cutting height and mow less frequently during hot dry spells.
- Leave the clippings on the grass to act as a mulch and replenish nutrients. Only rake them up if the grass was overly long when cut, or was wet and sticking together in large clumps.

Bee & Butterfly Gardens

Our relationship with the honey bee dates back to the advent of gardening, and the spring and summer wouldn't be the same without the sound of their industry.

MEDIEVAL MONKS WERE great beekeepers, harvesting honey as a sweetener and for making mead. Wax was used for candles and wood polish, and both honey and wax were important ingredients in the production of medicines. Generally, bees were housed in the kitchen garden or orchard to facilitate pollination of flowers. Unlike today's wooden beehives, the structures where bees were housed were made from woven wicker or straw, which had to be waterproofed or given extra cover from the elements. You sometimes see niches in old monastery walls where straw bee skeps were placed.

Aside from honey bees, many other bees and insects are involved in pollination and consequently in the production of seeds, fruits and berries. Ensuring that your garden has some nectar-producing blooms virtually year round will cater for all, including butterflies that wake up from hibernation too early. One of the first pollinators on the scene in spring is the bumble-bee, which busies itself with early fruit blossom and is the only insect heavy enough to prise open the flowers of broad (fava) beans. It also pollinates tomatoes, strawberries and raspberries. Bumble-bees like flowers that have easy access, such as wide-fluted bells or dish-shaped landing platforms, as well as plants that have many small flowers arranged in a dome or ball. They are particularly attracted by the colour blue and emerge from fluffy cardoon flowers covered in blue pollen. Watch out for them foraging among foxgloves, bellflowers (*Campanula*), borage, cranesbills, snapdragons, ornamental alliums and wild teasels.

LEFT: Including a wealth of colourful, nectar-bearing blooms in your garden all year round will encourage bees and butterflies.

ABOVE: Unlike honey bees, which can be enticed into beehives like the one illustrated, bumble-bees nest in underground crevices filled with a soft lining of collected moss, feathers and hair. Clay plant pots buried in a sunny bank with only the drainage hole visible, or old teapots with just the spout sticking out, may persuade new queens to nest. Fill with dried lawn cuttings, moss, hay or kapok.

ABOVE: Virtually all herbs that produce flowers are highly sought after by bees of every kind, but the flowers of marjoram, thyme, sage, lavender, lemon balm, mint and chives are especially attractive to them. The dilemma is that flowering has an adverse effect on the flavour of herb leaves, but you can compromise by harvesting leaves from the back of the plant and leaving the front ready to bloom.

Bees also love old-fashioned cottage flowers, especially those that are fragrant or aromatic. Watch the activity increase when you plant such bee attractors as catmint (*Nepeta*), bee balm (*Monarda*), Jacob's ladder (*Polemonium*), delphiniums, lupins and sweet peas. The petals of cranesbills are marked with prominent nectar guides, and there are many species to choose from, all of them popular with bees.

RIGHT: The gardener who is already catering for the nectar and pollen interests of bees will also be providing multi-coloured butterflies with plenty to feed on throughout the year. However, certain plants, particularly those with blue or purple flowers, seem irresistible to butterflies at particular times:

In spring, wallflowers, grape hyacinth (*Muscari*), aubrieta, honesty (*Lunaria annua*) and lilac (*Syringa*) offer heady fragrances to tempt butterflies. From early to midsummer, dame's violet (*Hesperis matronalis*), thrift (*Armeria maritima*), lavender and scabious catch their attention. Then from late summer, buddleia (the aptly

named butterfly bush), hebe, phlox, *Caryopteris* and Joe Pye weed (*Eupatorium purpureum*) offer valuable food stops, followed in autumn by hebe, ice plant (*Sedum spectabile*), calamint (*Calamintha*), Michaelmas daisy (*Aster*) and ivy (*Hedera*).

Butterflies and moths need nectar to sustain themselves and food plants for their caterpillars, as well as somewhere to roost or hibernate. Most require a specific native plant for breeding, so it is important to grow plenty of wildflowers, grasses and shrubs and to leave corners of the garden undisturbed, so that the butterfly population has a chance to thrive.

Winter Blooms

Gardeners have always treasured plants that flower during winter. By defying the elements, the delicate blooms appear nothing short of miraculous. They lift our spirits, reminding us that spring is waiting in the wings.

ONE FEATURE THAT many winter shrubs have in common is scent. This can be powerfully sweet and spicy or like an expensive French perfume, and on a still, warm day you'll often detect the fragrance some distance from its source. Make the most of these plants by placing them next to paths and doorways or by growing them in a sheltered courtyard.

Some spring-flowering bulbs and herbaceous plants can be coaxed to flower prematurely and brought into the house for decoration long before anything is stirring in the garden. Other plants need no special treatment – these are the true harbingers of spring. Frost or snow may damage their blooms, but such resilient plants usually have many buds in reserve.

LEFT: The beautiful scent of daphne pervades the winter garden.

RIGHT: Snowdrops and red-stemmed dogwood make perfect partners.

Sweet & Spicy Winter Flowers

The following winter-flowering shrubs are noted for their perfume. Many have been grown in cottage gardens for centuries.

- Laurustinus (*Viburnum tinus*)
- *Mahonia japonica*
- Mezereon (*Daphne mezereum*)
- Shrubby honeysuckle (*Lonicera* x *purpusii* 'Winter Beauty')
- Sweet box (*Sarcococca* species and varieties)
- *Viburnum farrari* (formerly *V. fragrans*)
- *Viburnum* x *bodnantense* (e.g. 'Dawn', 'Deben', 'Charles Lamont')
- Wintersweet (*Chimonanthus praecox*)
- Witch hazel (*Hamamelis mollis* 'Pallida')

ABOVE: The early flowers of camellias need protection from frost. Use old tea leaves as a mulch – tea is of the same genus and therefore supplies appropriate nutrients.

Early Spring Flowers

Most early bulbs and perennials are woodland plants, and like dappled shade and humus-rich soil. They will thrive beneath winter- or spring-flowering shrubs and trees. However, a few enjoy a sunny, well-drained position. Try the following:

- Crocus – early flowering (*C. chrysanthus* cultivars, e.g. 'Blue Pearl' and 'Cream Beauty'; *Crocus tommasinianus*) – full sun, well-drained soil
- Dwarf iris (e.g. *Iris reticulata* and cultivars) – full sun, well-drained soil
- Hellebore (e.g. *Helleborus orientalis* hybrids) – dappled shade, moist soil
- Lungwort (e.g. *Pulmonaria officinalis*) – dappled shade, moist soil
- Primrose and polyanthus (especially double-flowered 'Captain Blood' and 'Miss Indigo'; 'Guinevere' has purple foliage) – require moisture-retentive ground
- Snowdrop (*Galanthus nivalis* and *G. n.* 'Flore Pleno') – light shade, moist soil
- Sweet violet (*Viola odorata*) – full sun or light shade, medium soil
- Winter aconite (*Eranthis hyemalis*) – soak the shrivelled corms of aconite and anemone overnight before planting in full sun or light shade, medium soil

Orchard & Hedgerow

Flowers are pretty, but nothing beats the feeling of

permanence and the sheer beauty and structure of a

well-grown tree, even one of modest size.

Old-fashioned mixed hedgerows

add their own charm – especially when

laden with nuts and berries.

In country areas and on the outskirts of towns you can sometimes still see the remnants of an old orchard: a grouping of gnarled apple trees or perhaps a towering pear tree that no one has tended in years. Traditional orchards were abandoned for several reasons. One was advances in production, with varieties being grown on dwarfing rootstocks for machine cropping. Another was that improvements in storage and an influx of stock from countries overseas meant that people could buy apples, and other fruits that were normally seasonal, throughout the year.

Now, however, more and more people are thinking carefully about what they eat, particularly with regard to chemical sprays, and are beginning to grow their own fruits once again. It's certainly very satisfying when you can confidently walk up to a tree, pick off one of its sun-ripened fruits and bite into the juicy flesh! Another factor that favours home production is choice. At

Seek out old varieties from specialist growers so that you have a range of flavours to experience.

one time you'd encounter scores of different local varieties as you travelled round the country. In most places, sadly, pressure to produce more uniform crops, which withstand storage and transport, and fit the supermarkets' idea of what a particular fruit should look like, have caused local varieties, with characteristics such as unique flavour and frost resistance, to disappear.

If you have a spare corner of the garden that you don't have time to cultivate with neat lawns and flower borders, you might consider planting a few fruit trees – in effect making a mini orchard. Consult a specialist and plant varieties that taste good and are suited to your area. Alternatively, create a mini woodland, with a few small native trees, which will provide habitats for a wide range of wildlife.

A wildflower meadow is a perfect complement to a traditional orchard.

Plant your fences with wall shrubs and climbers to soften them.

Mow meandering paths through long grass so that you can enjoy the contrast between the flower-studded area and short turf.

It's best to keep the ground clear of grass and weeds below fruit trees – regular mulching with organic material will suppress weed germination, as well as improving the soil structure and fertility. With non-productive trees, though, you have the perfect conditions for naturalizing woodland flowers. In a few years, the area will have become a little haven of tranquillity both for you and the local wildlife. What is more, it will require far less attention than other parts of your plot.

The country-style hedgerow is another traditional feature that has much to recommend it. Unlike solid fences and walls that can create damaging turbulence, boundary hedges, punctuated with trees such as damson, filter the wind effectively. They also reduce noise far more efficiently than fences: an important factor if your garden borders a busy road. A mixed hedge of native plants supports a far wider range of birds, animals and insects than one created from exotic shrubs, and the plants will tend to have fewer cultivation problems. Provided it's trimmed once a year, and laid roughly every seven years, it will keep in good order, forming an impenetrable, productive and attractive barrier with an abundance of blossom, fruits, nuts and berries.

Garden hedges can also be shaped to add humour and design to the garden. In recent years, there has been a great resurgence of interest in the art of topiary, with garden centres stocking ready-clipped pieces. However, the somewhat quirky style of cottage topiary is easy to emulate as a beginner and needs only the most basic of tools – plus a little confidence!

Traditional Fruit-growing

Fruiting trees, bushes and shrubs have featured in gardens since ancient times. They are breathtaking when they blossom and just as evocative in autumn, when the apples, pears, cherries, plums and crab apples are ripening.

THE CAREFREE ATMOSPHERE of an old orchard is something that many gardeners would like to emulate in a corner of their modern gardens. If you have room, you could plant old varieties grafted on to rootstock that enables them to attain full size. These may take several years to bear fruit, and you could end up using a ladder for harvesting, but being able to walk or sit beneath the fruit-laden branches is magical. Where space is limited, however, especially when growing on fertile soils in particularly favourable areas, it may be better to select trees grown on semi-dwarfing rootstock.

Relatively little choice of fruit variety is offered at supermarkets, and selection is often based on appearance and handling properties rather than taste and texture. A good example is the russet apple, whose varieties are thought visually unappealing but which are juicy, with excellent flavour and good keeping qualities. The Victoria plum is another that is a 'must have' for home production. The fruits are beautiful and delicious. Old varieties are part of our heritage.

Certain varieties are well worth growing, either because of their outstanding flavour, or because they are suited to specific regions: late-flowering types, for example, perform better in colder areas, where frost would otherwise ruin fruit set.

ABOVE: When deciding what to grow, consider the size of the plot and the soil type, as well as specific climatic conditions, such as the last frost date, minimum winter temperatures or level of exposure. Seek local advice about the best regional varieties, preferred rootstocks and pollinators, or ask your supplier for guidance.

ABOVE: Old gardening texts are illustrated with a range of different ways of training top fruit, such as the pear pyramid shown here. As well as being highly ornamental, training trees saves valuable space and can therefore increase the productivity of your garden. Cropping is often improved and maintenance and harvesting, once training is complete, tends to be easier. You can buy frames from specialist growers to help you with the shaping process.

BELOW RIGHT: Another crop for the orchard is the cobnut (*Corylus avellana*) or filbert (*C. maxima*), the latter so named because the nuts ripen on St. Philibert's Day, August 22nd. It is possible to keep these plants small, which cannot be said of either the walnut – once valued for its oil, dye and nuts – or the sweet chestnut. Prune cobnuts and filberts during the flowering season to help disperse the pollen, but avoid branches bearing the inconspicuous female flowers.

ABOVE: Old-fashioned quinces add a wonderful, rich flavour to jams, jellies and many kinds of desserts.

From Blossom to Harvest

Traditional orchards are places where you can revel in the seasons and indulge your senses.
And even if the trees are coming to the end of their time, the atmosphere remains evocative.

FRUITS BEGIN TO ripen as autumn unfolds and the season ends with a mouth-watering harvest! Maintenance of the orchard is not very time-consuming and there's plenty of opportunity to just sit back and enjoy the changing scene.

Apply grease bands to trunks in mid-autumn, fitting them 1.2m/4ft above soil level, above the point where the tree stake is tied to the trunk. This prevents pests, such as winter moth caterpillars, and ants, which farm aphids, crawling up from the ground. In late autumn rake up loose mulch material, leaf litter and windfalls and pick off leftover fruits. Throw away or burn what you collect to prevent disease spread.

Winter is the best time to prune apples and pears to remove diseased, dead and damaged wood, as well as to shape trees and encourage development of fruiting spurs. Wrap the trunks and larger branches with hessian (burlap) sacking to attract over-wintering caterpillars, such as that of the codling moth. You might like to collect them to feed to your resident robin!

Alternatively, hang pheromone traps from the trees in late spring. Prune plums and cherries during the active growing season to avoid the risk of infection by silver leaf disease.

Winter is an ideal time for planting new trees, provided you avoid frosty periods. Proper preparation is essential

ABOVE: The sight of plums ripening on the branches reminds us that autumn is fast approaching.

to ensure years of successful cropping. Head gardeners used to insist that when their men dug holes for new trees they made them big enough to fit their spade in – lying flat!

RIGHT: When planting fruit trees, break up a large circle of soil (say, 1m/3ft) to at least a spade's depth. Dig in organic matter to improve the soil, and bonemeal (use latex gloves) to boost root growth. An old country method of planting involves throwing a handful or more of barley grains into the planting hole. The barley germinates under the roots, releasing warmth and growth hormones, which encourage the tree's establishment. Water with home-made nettle liquor before and after planting, and cover the bare ground with a thick mulch of shredded organic matter mixed with well-rotted manure.

ABOVE: To obtain larger fruits and to lessen the strain on young trees in good fruit-setting years, it is necessary to thin fruit clusters. Begin this process in early summer using sharp scissors or your thumb and forefinger, and finish off in midsummer after the natural early summer fruit drop. Water trees regularly in dry spells while the fruit is forming and to prevent early leaf fall, especially if the orchard has only recently been established.

LEFT & BELOW RIGHT: The best approach to pest and disease management in the orchard is to establish a natural balance. You can do this by mulching with organic matter and by applying home-made fertilizers rather than artificial ones. High nitrogen feeds, for example, should be avoided, since they promote foliage at the expense of fruit and may encourage certain diseases. Instead apply a strong mix of home-made comfrey and nettle liquor in spring, and, once the weather warms up, plant around the base with beneficial plants. These keep the soil cool and moist by trapping dew and preventing a hard cap from forming. They also release nutrients and substances that discourage pests. Try the following herbs, salads, cottage and wild plants: chives, ground ivy, mustard, nasturtium, phacelia, pot marigold, purslane, spinach and wallflower.

If you have time, protect individual fruits that are approaching ripeness by tying on muslin (cheesecloth) bags. These prevent attack from wasps and birds.

The Garden Floor

In recent years, more and more people have been discovering the pleasure of creating a 'wild' garden. It is a wonderful way of bringing nature closer to home.

Creating a semi-wild area in your garden, whether a patch of flower-studded, grassy meadow or a mini woodland with naturalized bulbs and other flowers beneath the trees, will attract all manner of birds and other fascinating wildlife, and can feel like bringing a little bit of the countryside to your doorstep.

In a grassy meadow, if the area is large enough, you could mow meandering paths so that you can enjoy the contrast between the long meadow grass and short turf. Long grass is difficult to maintain with an ordinary lawnmower but can be cut with a brush cutter.

ABOVE: Woodland plants such as primroses relish dappled shade.

RIGHT: Relax and contemplate, sitting beneath a tree.

BELOW: One of the easiest ways to create a wild meadow effect is simply to allow the grass to grow long, cutting it just once a year at the end of summer. You'll be surprised how many wild species begin to appear if you delay cutting until after the majority have seeded. You can also try different mowing regimes to favour particular groups of wild flowers. For summer meadow flowers, mow until late spring and resume mowing in late summer. On rich soils, however, coarse grasses could dominate and you will need to reduce soil fertility by regular mowing and removal of cuttings to the compost heap. Another option is to remove the turf and start from scratch by re-sowing using a specialist mix of fine grasses, such as the fragrant sweet vernal grass, and wild flowers.

Weeds of the cornfields, including field poppies, ox-eye daisies, corncockle, corn marigold and cornflower, work well in sunny sites, attracting a range of beneficial insects; red campion, cowslip and the bumble-bee favourite, foxglove, prefer dappled shade. The latter is traditionally grown beneath apples to improve their keeping quality. In subsequent years you can add further variety to your wildflower patch using plug plants or seedlings that you've raised yourself.

Establishing Woodland Bulbs

Some bulbs naturalize readily in the grass under trees. They flower early in the year when the tree canopy has not fully established.

1 Plant in swathes of the same variety, either using a bulb planter for single bulbs, or, for larger areas, lifting the turf and grouping several in one spot.

2 Try clumps of miniature daffodils (*Cyclamineus* types), because they naturalize well and resemble the wild daffodil or Lent lily (*Narcissus pseudonarcissus*).

3 Plant snowdrops on ground that is moisture-retentive. Though temperamental, if they are happy they will multiply steadily.

4 Try other woodland bulbs that spread to form carpets, including snakeshead fritillaries (*Fritillaria meleagris*), wood anemones (*Anemone nemorosa*), wild garlic or ramsons, and English bluebells (*Hyacinthoides non-scripta*). If possible, plant snowdrops and bluebells 'in the green'.

5 Cut the grass where bulbs are growing once the foliage has turned yellow, but certainly no less than six weeks after the last flowering.

6 For larger bulbs, such as daffodils, nip off fading heads to prevent the plant wasting the following year's flowering resources on seed production.

ABOVE: Some nurseries offer select bulbs in active growth, or 'in the green'. Fresh bulbs, lifted after flowering, with a healthy set of leaves and strong roots establish much more readily than dry bulbs planted in the autumn.

Hedgerows & Boundaries

Planting a traditional mixed hedge of native species has many advantages. Thorny subjects, such as hawthorn, blackthorn, sweet briar, bramble and holly, help to make an impenetrable barrier that keeps out unwelcome visitors.

LEFT: Deciduous hedges add greatly to the beauty of the garden whatever the season, providing a living boundary that changes subtly through the year. To benefit wildlife, grow a mixed hedge using mainly native species and don't overclip.

BIRDS WILL BE grateful for a hedge's prickly protection, and roost and nest there in safety. Plants and animals that once lived on the margins of forests find hedges an acceptable substitute, and the large amount of foodstuff that a properly managed hedge produces sustains all manner of creatures, including small mammals such as dormice and several species of butterfly and moth. At one time people regularly supplemented their diet with hedgerow produce. Wild rosehip syrup, made from the real thing, is one of the richest sources of Vitamin C.

Another feature of the country hedge is that it is ever-changing, and is attractive for many months of the year. At the end of winter, hazel catkins dangle in the wind; in early spring, the frothy white blossom of blackthorn is one of the season's most uplifting sights, along with that of damson and wild cherry. A haze of apple-green hawthorn leaves is followed by creamy late spring blossom, and the elder, with its lacy tiers, also looks splendid. For weeks in summer the sweet briar and honeysuckle bear beautiful, fragrant flowers. Autumn sees a wealth of fruits, nuts and berries, and in winter, holly, yew and wild privet provide welcome greenery. When the frost arrives, even the bare twigs have a sculptural quality.

Establishing a Hedgerow

You can buy inexpensive 'country' mixtures of bare-root hedgerow plants in winter.

1 Dig a strip of land about 1m/1yd wide thoroughly, incorporating plenty of organic matter, such as well-rotted manure.

2 Plant two-year-old seedlings at a density of around five plants per metre/yard. Slope the plants at a 45 degree angle along the line of the hedge.

3 Cut plants back by about a third to encourage dense side shooting.

4 Mulch with a thick layer of manure or bark to retain moisture and suppress weeds. The following winter, cut the hedge back again but not quite so hard, and it will fill out.

SUITABLE HEDGEROW PLANTS

- Blackthorn (*Prunus spinosa*) – has early blossom and fruits, known as sloes, used for making sloe gin
- Dog rose (*Rosa canina*) – has scented pink or white flowers and red hips
- Dogwood (*Cornus sanguinea*) – has dark red winter stems
- Elder (*Sambucus nigra*) – has creamy, scented blossom and black berries used to make wine
- Field maple (*Acer campestre*) – has red-tinged young leaves in spring
- Guelder rose (*Viburnum opulus*) – has flowers, fruit and autumn colour
- Hawthorn (*Crataegus monogyna*) – use for approximately 70 per cent of the total hedge has bright new foliage, blossom and red haws)
- Hazel (*Corylus avellana*) – has catkins and cobnuts
- Holly (*Ilex aquifolium*) – has evergreen foliage and red berries on female plants
- Sweet briar or eglantine (*Rosa eglanteria*) – has scented foliage and flowers, and red hips
- Wild privet (*Ligustrum vulgare*) – has scented cream flowers and evergreen foliage

ABOVE: To increase the windbreak potential of your hedge, allow individual plants, such as hawthorn, field maple, holly and yew, to grow as trees. You could also plant a number of other trees within or adjacent to the hedgerow. Wild cherry (*Prunus avium*) and wild crab (*Pyrus malus*) are grown for their blossom and fruits, while the damson (*Prunus insititia*) yields a harvest used for wines, jams and pies.

ABOVE: The elder is known as the 'medicine chest of the countryside'. Its flowers, fruit, leaves and bark all have medicinal uses, one of the most common being a remedy for colds and flu. The name 'elder' derives from the belief that the plant promotes long life, but take care when harvesting: according to folklore, a dryad or 'elder mother' inhabits the tree, and her permission is needed before so much as a leaf is taken!

Topiary

The art of topiary was probably first practised by the Romans, and interest in it has waxed and waned through the centuries according to the vagaries of fashion.

COUNTRY-DWELLERS WERE always quick to copy and adapt ideas from the great country houses, and topiary was no exception. Although yew, *Phillyrea* and box were the principal plants being used up at the Big House, ordinary folk discovered that they could also shape their own hedging plants and evergreens including holly, laurustinus (*Viburnum tinus*), aromatic myrtle (*Myrtus communis*), sweet bay (*Laurus nobilis*) and the quick-growing privet.

Well-maintained hedges were essential for keeping the household's own livestock contained, as well as for preventing animals in the surrounding fields from breaking into the garden. The practice of hedge-laying was once commonplace, but machines have now largely taken over cutting. To rejuvenate an old hedge, the thick bare stems are chopped through sufficiently to bend them down at a shallow angle, and this near-horizontal position causes the sap to flow more readily and stimulate dormant buds to spring to life. The resulting shoots are vertical and grow in great density.

ABOVE: You can really let your imagination run riot with topiary, as these billowing box formations demonstrate. Simple, abstract designs are relatively easy for a beginner to tackle.

LEFT: Clip topiary using sheep shears, or, for precision clipping of small and complex shapes, use small 'ladies' shears' with a fine, pointed nose. For large simple shapes, use regular hand shears or a powered hedge trimmer. When shaping holly or bay standards, use secateurs (pruners) to avoid unsightly half-cut leaves. It's also best to use secateurs when making the first tentative shaping cuts, for example, a spiral.

Simple Shapes

The easiest topiary forms to clip are domes. You can achieve almost instant results by clipping shrubs that already have a rounded habit, such as box (Buxus sempervirens), Hebe rakaiensis *or shrubby honeysuckle* (Lonicera nitida).

1 If you are beginning with a large shrub, cut away any excess foliage that doesn't fit the shape you want to create. If possible, stand over the plant and turn your shears upside down so that the angle of the blades follows the curve that you are creating.

2 Gradually clip off shallow layers of foliage. Walk around the shape and stand back regularly to check on your progress. Make sure the shape is symmetrical on all sides. The dome is an ideal form because foliage receives good light top to bottom.

Training Standards

The standard, a form of topiary where a shaped head is supported by a smooth stem, has long been popular, and you'll see numerous examples made from evergreen and flowering shrubs, small trees and even shrubby herbs, such as rosemary. Myrtle and holly were always popular choices with country-dwellers in the past.

1 Take a young plant or seedling and attach a cane to the main stem to keep it straight as it grows.

2 Remove any side branches at this stage, but allow some foliage to grow on the stem during training, as this helps to strengthen it.

3 When the plant has grown to just below the required height, pinch out the shoot tip. This encourages a proliferation of branches at the top, which can be clipped or cut to shape.

4 Pinch off leaves on the stem to create a clean leg.

Kitchen Garden

Seeing an array of delicious homegrown ingredients

on your plate is immensely satisfying. The taste and

texture of freshly gathered fruits and vegetables

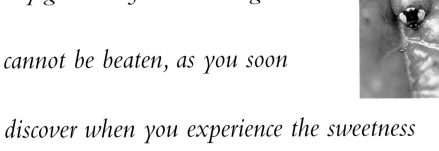

cannot be beaten, as you soon

discover when you experience the sweetness

of peas eaten straight from the pod.

In the past, the weather and the seasons had the strongest influence on when people carried out cultivation, sowing, planting and harvesting. Since ancient times, the phases of the moon and the movements of the planets have also been guiding garden activities. However, despite such celestial assistance, wise gardeners are also practical and a touch fatalistic. Aware of nature's unpredictability, they often hedge their bets, and hold plants in reserve to cover possible losses. The gardener who wrote this rhyme had clearly had a few disappointments: 'Sow one for the rook, one for the crow, one to die and one to grow'.

You are bound to lose a few plants to pests and diseases but if you raise fruit and vegetables using organic methods, maintaining the soil's fertility and establishing a natural balance between predator and prey, you shouldn't have too many problems. The taste of fresh home-grown produce is often much better than supermarket fare, and you can be confident that it is free of harmful chemicals. These days commercial production of salads

Don't put tender vegetables out too early – keep a close watch on the weather.

and vegetables often takes place in the controlled environment of glass houses, forcing unnaturally rapid cropping. In some cases hydroponic, soil-less technology ensures that plants get the nutrients and water they need to grow well, but they may not develop flavour. Tomatoes and strawberries often end up tasting watery because of the way they have been produced. Looking after your soil has multiple benefits, from maintaining good structure and drainage to promoting a healthy and beneficial population of microbes and minibeasts. Another plus factor is that the trace elements, essential nutrients and other natural substances supplied by organic soil additives (including well-rotted manure, garden compost, leaf mould and comfrey or nettle liquor) ensure that fruits and vegetables have the added extras that make them tastier than produce grown solely with the aid of chemical fertilizers.

Lettuce and baby spinach can be sown in succession.

Protect vulnerable seedlings with cloches on cold nights.

Move a scarecrow around occasionally to ensure that it is effective.

The taste of organic, home-grown vegetables cannot be beaten.

Everything tastes best when really fresh, and the time fruit, vegetables and herbs spend in transit from farm to supermarket can have quite a marked effect on flavour. Even organically grown supermarket produce suffers compared to plants taken straight from the garden and eaten or cooked immediately. To make the most of limited space, grow plants that benefit from being raised on well-fed ground and served straight from the garden – strawberries including the aromatic fraises des bois; little sun-warmed cherry tomatoes; cut and come again lettuce varieties; mangetouts (snow peas); hot, peppery rocket (arugula); baby corn;

asparagus and globe artichokes grown to the size of golf balls, quartered and sautéed so they're still succulent.

You can also grow a range of varieties rarely seen in the shops, such as scorzonera, cardoon and blanched sea kale as well as other taste sensations such as chicory (Belgian endive), purple sprouting broccoli and Florence fennel. And by close planting or early cropping you can grow delicious mini or bite-size vegetables without paying the usual premium – baby carrots, kohlrabi and cauliflowers so small that you can eat a whole head in a single serving; salad potatoes and mini courgettes (zucchini).

A Potager

Potagers are formal kitchen gardens, designed for looks as well as productivity. If you don't have space for a dedicated kitchen garden, why not devote just one bed to a selection of attractive salad greens, fruits or herbs.

POTAGERS OFFER THE gardener the chance to design an ever-changing kitchen garden with artistic licence. Here is a garden that makes the most of the ornamental qualities of vegetables, herbs and fruit. Potagers have great appeal, turning the vegetable area into a decorative feature. With a geometric layout of beds often bordered with low evergreen hedging or traditional barley-twist tiles, and intersected by pathways, potagers usually have a centrepiece too, perhaps a pyramid-trained pear tree or a metal gazebo festooned with a hardy grape vine.

Planning how you're going to plant up a potager can be fun. Some crops, such as lettuce and strawberries, are good for edging or growing in rows, while others, such as the sprawling courgettes (zucchini) and squashes, are more practical in blocks. Runner (green) beans and climbing French beans need support and work best if grown up cane wigwams.

ABOVE: You will need to operate at least the most basic crop rotation system to avoid the build-up of pests and diseases. Keeping a record of what you plant where each year will help you to plan.

40

Making Raised Beds

This technique has been practised since medieval times and has much to recommend it to today's gardener. The extra depth of soil allows easier cultivation of heavy ground, such as clay, which has a tendency to become waterlogged over winter and is slow to warm up in spring.

1 Mark out the shape of the beds and pathways and roughly prepare the beds. Skim topsoil off the proposed pathways and heap it up on to the beds.

2 Hammer a stout, pointed timber stake into the ground at each of the four corners of the bed. Pre-drill holes close to each end of four lengths of thick tanalized gravel boards. Hammer them in place on to the stakes, using galvanized ring shank nails.

3 Spread the soil out to fill the frame, at the same time mixing in plenty of well-rotted manure.

4 Excavate the pathways to accommodate a layer of rammed hardcore and top with decorative gravel.

Ornamental Produce

Certain vegetables and fruits are delightfully ornamental and, when they are mixed with herbs and edible flowers in simple patterns, the end result can be every bit as decorative as a parterre filled with bedding. Try the following:

- Apples and pears, trained into ornamental shapes
- Blueberries
- Cardoon
- Cherry tomatoes, e.g. 'Gardeners' Delight'
- Courgettes (zucchini) (esp. yellow-fruited)
- Curly kale
- Florence fennel
- Globe artichoke
- Leeks
- Purple- and yellow-podded French beans
- Red cabbage
- Red oak leaf lettuce and others with coloured or ornamental leaves
- Red or white currants (these can be trained as space-saving cordons)
- Ruby chard (and other coloured chards)
- Runner (green) beans with red flowers, or the old-fashioned, pink- and white-flowered varieties such as 'Painted Lady'
- Squashes and pumpkins
- Strawberries
- Winter cabbage

BELOW: Decorative brickwork paths laid with a herringbone or basket-weave design create an old-fashioned atmosphere in the potager or ornamental kitchen garden. If possible, try to get hold of reclaimed bricks from an architectural salvage yard, but make sure the bricks are frost-proof, or they will start to break up during the winter. Settle the bricks in by hand, using a rubber mallet rather than a mechanized plate vibrator. You don't want the path to be too perfect – a few lumps and bumps, and a well-worn look, will add interest and character!

Sowing, Planting & Harvesting

Gardening activities are normally timed according to the weather or, more broadly, to coincide with the seasons. Sowing and planting begin in spring and we reap the rewards of our labours during the autumn harvest.

BY OBSERVING THE seasons, the activity of plants and animals, and local weather patterns, people in the past were able to determine the best time to sow, plant or reap.

According to an ancient tradition, the moon has a significant role in the gardening calendar. People recognized that the moon affected the tides, and believed that, since plants are largely made up of water, the moon must also influence their growth and development. Between the new moon and the half-full moon, in the first quarter, plant annuals, especially leafy plants, such as cabbage, celery, endive and spinach. From the half-full moon to the full moon in the second quarter, plant annuals that are vines and produce seed inside the fruit, such as beans and peas, peppers, squash, courgette (zucchini), aubergine (eggplant), tomato and cucumber. Garlic and melons can be planted in both these quarters. From the full moon to the half-full moon, in the third quarter, plant biennials, perennials, bulbs, root crops, and crops for over-wintering, such as onions, potatoes, rhubarb, grapes and berrying plants. This is a good time to plant trees and shrubs. From the half-full moon to the new moon, in the final quarter, carry out maintenance jobs, such as cutting back and clearing the ground, turning the soil over, weeding and pest control.

ABOVE: Collecting your own seed is thrifty, can be very rewarding and allows you to grow plants free from pesticides from start to finish. Store the seeds in a paper bag placed in a sealed container in a cool dark place until they are needed.

LEFT: Sow seed evenly over the surface of firm and damp potting mix.

Autumn Harvest for the Winter Kitchen

Certain vegetables can be stored for use through the winter until fresh stocks are available in spring.
Traditional storage methods can keep produce in good condition for a surprisingly long time.

- Ripen pumpkins and squashes in the sun so that they can be stored successfully. Raise off the ground slightly during ripening to prevent slug damage and rotting and to allow free air circulation.

- Pull onions and leave on the ground to ripen once the tops start to die back and fall over. If the weather is wet, dry them on wooden racks or in netting hammocks. Don't try storing thick-necked onions.

- Prepare onions, shallots and garlic for storage, braiding the dried leaves on to a length of rope or twine.

- Hang up winter cabbage in netting bags.

- Dry beans by suspending whole plants, complete with pods, in an airy environment.

- In relatively mild areas without deep penetrating frosts, leave swedes (rutabagas), parsnips, carrots and potatoes in the ground until needed. For convenience, e.g. in rainy weather, keep a small store ready-lifted.

- For convenience lift a few root crops, such as beetroot (beets) and carrots, and store in boxes of slightly moist peat (peat substitute).

BELOW: It's well known in country kitchens that parsnips and Brussels sprouts don't develop their sweet flavour until after exposure to frost. The Brussels sprouts at the bottom of the stem mature first, so harvest from that end, but don't leave them to get too large or they will become tough and lose their delicate flavour. If severe frost occurs, pull the whole plant up immediately afterwards and store in an unheated garage or outhouse.

LEFT: Pea seeds can take a long time to germinate in cold ground in spring, falling prey to mice. You can try rolling the seeds in paraffin to make them unpalatable or try the following old gardening tip. Sow the seeds in the greenhouse, in drainage pipes that have been cut in half, or plastic guttering, filled with compost. When the seedlings are 5cm/2in tall, harden them off and then slide the contents of the pipe into a ready-prepared drill. This avoids any setback due to root disturbance.

Early Crops & Tender Fruits

Those gardeners lucky enough to have a garden surrounded by high walls are aware of the benefits of creating a favourable microclimate, allowing for virtual year-round production of fruit and vegetables.

VICTORIAN HEAD GARDENERS were known for their ingenuity and used many techniques to extend the growing season and to raise tender crops. One feature common at the time and still in use, at least until the 1930s, was the hot bed. This was essentially a pile of fresh manure that was shaped, covered with a layer of loam and fitted with a special glass-topped frame. The heat generated by the decomposing material enabled all kinds of vegetables, salads and flowers to be raised ahead of the normal growing season. It was essentially the forerunner of the heated propagator.

The scope of Victorian fruit- and vegetable-growing was broadened with the mass production of lightweight glazing bars for glass buildings. However, even without the extra protection of a lean-to glasshouse, sunny walls can produce enough heat to ensure crops of tender or early blossoming fruits, including figs, apricots, peaches, nectarines, almonds and pears. Another advantage to wall cultivation is that you can protect peaches and almonds from peach leaf

curl. Cover trees with a clear plastic 'lean-to', open at the ends, from autumn (after leaf fall) till early spring, to keep rain off – this prevents the spread of fungal spores.

ABOVE: With careful planning you can raise all manner of tender fruits and vegetables with the aid of a greenhouse and a cold frame, as well as extending the cropping season of a wide variety of salads and herbs from early spring into winter.

Forcing Crops

Special clay pots were once commonly used to force tender, pink shoots of certain varieties of rhubarb early in the season. Witloof chicory (Belgian endive), endive and sea kale, a delicious vegetable grown for its long blanched stems, may also be forced or blanched to rid the edible parts of bitterness. To force rhubarb:

1 Choose a variety suitable for early cropping, such as the old favourites 'Timperley Early' or 'Hawkes Champagne'.

2 Cover the dormant crowns with forcing pots or large buckets in midwinter, packing round the crown with straw. Traditional rhubarb forcers have a small lid that can be removed to check on progress.

3 Harvest in early spring for delicious stems, which are markedly less acidic.

4 If you don't have a rhubarb forcing pot, simply cover the crown with a thick layer of straw. Secure with netting to stop it blowing away.

Growing Fruit in Pots

Even without a warm, sunny wall on which to train tender fruits, you can grow them successfully in pots.

Peaches, apricots and nectarines can be kept small by being grafted on to dwarfing or miniaturizing rootstocks. Protect them in the greenhouse over winter, and then stand them out on the patio once the leaves have expanded. The early spring blossoms will need to be pollinated by hand to ensure fruit set.

Figs are grown on their own roots, and if their roots are unrestricted they will grow enormous before bearing fruit, so they are good candidates for pots. 'Brown Turkey' and 'Brunswick' are the hardiest cultivars, but if you do bring them under cover in winter you'll also be able to grow the delectable old French varieties, such as 'Violette Dauphine', 'Bourjassotte Grise' and 'Negro Largo'. Potted figs may be over-wintered in a dark shed or garage, since they lose their leaves in winter and don't require light. Wrap the pots and stems with hessian (burlap) packed with straw for extra insulation.

ABOVE: Growing fruit trees against a wall in any shape is efficient. Training stems closer to horizontal increases the flow of sap, resulting in a good yield. It takes 3–4 years to achieve a good basic structure on a peach or almond fan.

Once established, you need to maintain the basic structure. In the middle of spring remove any shoots growing out from the wall, as well as weak or congested side shoots or laterals. After harvest you also need to cut the fruited stem back to a replacement lateral, which will flower the following spring.

Natural Defences

In the kitchen garden there are many simple cultivation techniques you can use to help prevent pest and disease problems; the key to success is to provide the kind of conditions that promote strong, healthy growth.

M ANY GARDENERS HAVE abandoned traditional methods of pest control in favour of a 'quick fix' solution for any problems that arise. We now know, however, that the use of chemicals can have unfortunate consequences. For example, slug and snail poisons lead to birds such as song thrushes eating the dead pests, and being poisoned in their turn. Similarly, if you spray paths with weedkiller, you may inadvertently kill nesting bumblebees. Sticking to organic methods allows the natural predators of pests to build up, so that pest attacks become less serious.

Mixing different types of plants together in small batches in the garden is beneficial, because it is more difficult for pests to focus on their target, and some plant combinations actively deter pests. The 'companion' plant either provides protection or boosts the other's growth in some way. A good example is the potato, which provides mutual benefits when grown with sunflower, dead nettle (*Lamium*), nasturtium, cabbage, sweetcorn or peas. Alternating rows of potatoes with broad (fava) beans deters insect pests, and a horseradish plant at each corner of the plot is said to promote healthy growth. Planting sage between rows of cabbage deflects egg-laying butterflies; planting onions and scorzonera between carrots confuses carrot root fly, and French marigold (*Tagetes patula*) kills eelworm, a serious soil-borne pest of potatoes.

RIGHT: You can now buy a range of artificial habitats to encourage beneficial insects, including ladybird (ladybug) and bumble-bee houses and the 'lacewing hotel' pictured.

BELOW: Rather than getting into the habit of routine spraying, use disease-resistant strains and follow the age-old system of crop rotation, which helps prevent the depletion of nutrients and the build-up of pests and diseases. During the growing season, and from year to year, swap rows or small blocks of plants belonging to the same group with other plants belonging to different groups. Some groups, such as the brassicas – broccoli, cabbage, kale – are more susceptible to pests and diseases, while others have advantageous characteristics. Cucurbits, including courgettes (zucchini) and squashes, together with potatoes, smother the ground and are excellent for 'cleaning' a weedy patch; legumes – the peas and beans – have nitrogen-fixing root nodules that increase the fertility of the soil; and members of the onion family ward off a variety of pests and diseases.

Companion Planting

Certain mixtures of vegetables and herbs, when planted together, are said to be favourable to the growing conditions of each other. Others have a detrimental effect on growth and texture. 'Dry' herbs, such as rosemary and lavender, can make vegetables like lettuce and cucumber less juicy, while lettuce makes radishes go soft.

GOOD COMPANION PLANTS:

- Beans with beetroot (beets) (but not climbing beans), cabbage, carrots, cauliflower, celery, cucumber, leeks or sweetcorn
- Beetroot with dwarf beans, kohlrabi or onions
- Cabbages with beans, parsley, hyssop, mint or sage
- Carrots with onions, rosemary or scorzonera
- Cucumber with beans, potatoes, sweetcorn, sunflowers, dill, kohlrabi
- Kohlrabi interspersed with lettuce or Savoy cabbage
- Lettuce with baby carrots or dill
- Onions with dill
- Peas with radishes
- Strawberries with borage, dwarf beans, lettuce or spinach
- Tomatoes with parsley or pot marigolds

COMBINATIONS TO AVOID:

- Beans with onions or kohlrabi
- Beetroot with tomatoes
- Cabbages with onions or marjoram
- Parsley with cabbages or lettuce
- Potatoes with onions or orache
- Radishes with lettuce
- Red cabbages with tomatoes
- Tomatoes with kohlrabi, fennel or potatoes

Feeding the Soil

Wise gardeners know that the structure and fertility of the soil is the most important factor in raising plants successfully. Strong-growing plants are much less likely to suffer problems.

S OIL IS A COMPLEX living entity, and should never be left bare for any length of time, because structure and fertility may be damaged. A handful of earth teems with millions of micro-organisms, which work to break down organic matter and release its nutrients.

Topsoil, the term given to the uppermost layers that are capable of supporting plant growth, varies greatly in depth, depending on environmental conditions and the care the soil has received. In ground that has been cultivated and dressed with compost and manure over the years, the topsoil is deep and dark in colour, indicating a high humus content.

Manure is obtainable from farms or riding schools – it must be well rotted before use. Home-made compost and leaf mould will also improve your soil. Alternatively grow green manures on

temporarily vacated ground. Woody material, such as stems and twigs from pruning, can be shredded and spread over the beds as a weed-suppressing, moisture-retentive mulch. This eventually breaks down to be incorporated into the topsoil by worms and other organisms.

ABOVE: For winter mulching, use 3–4-year old stable manure, dark with a rough texture. On sandy soils, spread it in late winter, as a thick, moisture-retentive mulch. On clay, turn it into the topsoil.

LEFT: Compost made from recycled garden and kitchen waste is an excellent soil conditioner.

ABOVE: The leaves of the herb comfrey, particularly those of a form of Russian comfrey called 'Bocking 14', are rich in nutrients. When broken down and diluted with water, they make an excellent liquid feed. Spring-picked nettles can also be used. Fill a barrel with water and suspend a sack of freshly cut material within it for four weeks. Drain off the resultant liquid as required and compost the residue. Alternatively, raise a container on bricks and drill a hole in the base. Fill the container with weighted-down and compressed leaves. Collect the thick dark liquor that seeps out. Dilute 10–20 times.

BELOW: Green manures replenish soil and keep bare earth covered between cropping and over winter. Some, such as alfalfa, field bean and various clovers, have nitrogen-fixing nodules on their roots. Plants such as the quick-growing mustard and phacelia are kept for just a few weeks, while others, including alfalfa, may be left for up to two years. Green manures such as grazing rye are also used on uncultivated ground. Chop up soft sappy growth to encourage wilting and fork into the soil, or hoe off the tops of annuals and leave on the surface.

BELOW: To make leaf mould, collect autumn leaves and either pack into black plastic bags pierced with holes or fill large chicken-wire containers. The material rots down to form a wonderful soil conditioner in one to two years.

Perfect Compost

Making your own compost is very satisfying. Home-made compost is ready once you are unable to identify its individual components. Growing nettles around the base of the compost heap is said to accelerate the rotting process.

1 Stand the compost bin on bare earth.

2 Put a layer of twiggy stems at the bottom to allow air to penetrate the heap. Add kitchen waste, such as vegetable peelings, annual weeds, grass clippings and shredded prunings in thin, alternating layers.

3 Do not add perennial weeds or those that have gone to seed. The heap may not get hot enough to kill them.

4 Don't allow the material to become too wet – keep the lid on the compost bin or cover with old carpet.

5 Water the compost if it becomes too dry to rot down.

6 To accelerate breakdown, turn the compost periodically to mix in oxygen. Either empty out the bin completely and refill it or turn the compost into an empty container.

Caring for Tools

Gardeners' tools are old, familiar friends. They should be ideally suited to the task in hand, comfortable to use and bearing the signs of years of faithful service.

W HEN PROPERLY CARED FOR, tools can be handed down through the generations to become part of a family's heritage. The blade of an old spade may be worn away to half its original length, the corners rounded through digging and regular sharpening, but rather than discarding worn items, wise gardeners invariably find them jobs for which they seem perfectly designed. Over the years, the shed wall acquires all manner of implements, lovingly maintained and repaired. Every craftsperson takes pride in the tools of their trade and good gardeners are no exception.

At one time, hand tools, such as shears, forks and scythes, would have been made to order by the local blacksmith; it is not uncommon to find personal touches among antique pieces, such as a turned wooden handle on a trowel. Even today's mass manufactured equipment can have its appeal, and once a gardener discovers a tool that feels right in the hands, is well balanced and in the right proportions to the body, they may be very reluctant to part with it.

LEFT: If you can take apart a pair of secateurs (pruners), it makes maintenance so much easier. With spare parts and a good care regime, there's no reason not to have the same pair for many years.

RIGHT: Some of the garden tools of yesteryear seem rather curious or cumbersome, while others are very similar to the ones we all use today. Clean and oil lightly after use to prevent rust.

Digging & Weeding Tools

Tools that come into contact with soil must be cleaned after use – never leave them in the ground or they will rust.

1 Non-stick, stainless-steel items can be wiped over with a cloth.

2 When mud is caked on, remove it using an old paint-stripping scraper or make one by cutting off the round end of an old spoon and flattening it with a hammer.

3 Finish cleaning with a stiff hand brush and cloth.

4 Wipe over the metal with an oily rag to prevent rust.

5 From time to time, sharpen the leading edge of the blades of hoes and spades. Clamp the tool into a vice and use a metal file to sharpen the upper edge only.

Cutting Tools

Sharp blades for hedging and lawn-edging shears, knives and secateurs (pruners) are essential for clipping, cutting or pruning, and reduce the risk of damage to plants. Cleaning tools after use makes the cutting action smoother.

1 Wipe the tool dry and remove debris with a cloth. Lightly sand the blades with emery paper or wire (steel) wool to remove sticky, dried-on sap.

2 Wipe over with an oily rag to prevent rust.

3 Check the tension of hinged cutting tools and tighten or loosen for comfort of use. Apply a couple of drops of lubricating oil to the nut or spring to prevent stiffness.

4 To sharpen knife blades, moisten an oilstone with a few drops of oil.

5 Sharpen the side without the thumbnail indentation first. Move the blade over the stone, keeping it flat, and using a circular motion.

6 Turn the blade over and, making sure that you keep it at a 25° angle to the stone, sharpen the edge with repeated strokes, pushing the blade first forwards and then lightly drawing it back.

ABOVE: Store all garden tools under cover, in a dry place. If you hang them on a wall rack, or on conveniently positioned hooks or nails, it helps to keep the shed tidy and means you can easily see where they are.

Herb Garden

Working in a herb garden is more of a treat than a chore. You will experience the powerful aroma of leaves crushed underfoot, and the slightest disturbance will release fragrant oils. With all those flavours to choose from, your cooking will be transformed.

The appeal of herbs has endured for centuries. In recent years, there has been a tremendous resurgence of interest in growing and using herbs for culinary, cosmetic, household and other purposes. The range of herbal and back-to-nature body-care products is vast, and the use of plant-based and homeopathic remedies has increased dramatically.

It's fascinating to learn about the old names and former uses of herbs, and it makes you realize the extent to which they were a part of everyday life. A good example is the little, white-flowered milfoil, whose Anglo-Saxon name is yarrow. The plant we now know as an irksome lawn weed was once hung in bunches on the back of the shed door, which might seem a curious custom until you discover that yarrow's long-forgotten names are 'bloodwort', 'sanguinary' and 'staunchgrass'. It seems that gardeners of old were simply being practical, having first aid on hand in case

Common and purple-leaved sage and catmint make wonderfully scented edges for borders.

of accidents with tools! The more you find out about the ancient heritage of herbs, the more you feel yourself becoming drawn into another world. When you plant a herb seat or a chamomile lawn, or mark out the complex pattern of a knot garden, you're following the traditions of an earlier era.

Traditional herb gardens can involve quite a lot of work. Chamomile lawns, for example, need meticulous weeding, and box hedges and knots must be clipped to maintain their neat profile. The traditional time to clip box is at the end of spring or beginning of summer when the risk of frost scorching the soft re-growth is minimal.

Most people know how to make use of popular culinary and aromatic herbs, but have little or no experience with medicinal herbs. When we incorporate old cottage flowers

Carpeting plants, especially the many varieties of creeping thyme, release their fragrant oils if stepped on, and are ideal for planting pathways.

The poisonous foxglove is a powerful medicinal herb and is popular with bumble-bees.

into planting schemes, we are often unwittingly growing medicinal herbs. Some, such as German chamomile, which helped induce sleep; comfrey, grown for its soothing and anti-inflammatory qualities; feverfew, which was used to treat headaches; and the humble, pot marigold (*Calendula*), which was used to heal skin wounds, have become better known of late, but who would suspect periwinkle, mallow, cowslip, dead nettle or forget-me-not?

Whether you create a herb garden for culinary, medicinal and household use, or simply grow a selection because you enjoy their appearance or aroma, herbs are guaranteed to give you pleasure. They also offer the additional benefit of attracting many appealing insects, including butterflies. As the new herb gardener soon appreciates, the humming of the bees at work in summer can be as soothing as the sound of a trickling fountain.

Traditional Designs

Gardens created exclusively for the cultivation of herbs often have a timeless quality. Flowers and foliage are understated, with a predominance of quiet colours, such as purples, blues, greens and white.

THE DESIGN OF THE TRADITIONAL HERB GARDEN was based on simple geometry, which engenders a feeling of ordered calm. The plants and materials used in construction may have changed over time, but formal, clipped hedging in yew or box, and solid paved paths of stone or brick, continue to be popular.

When choosing a design, consider the types of plants you wish to grow and their purpose. Do you want to crop herbs for the kitchen or do you simply want to sit and enjoy being surrounded by fragrant and aromatic plants? Herbs are not always well behaved and most need plenty of space. Some seed like fury, while others, including mints, lemon balm, tansy and comfrey, are rampant spreaders. Angelica, fennel and elecampane grow tall, the latter having a tendency to sprawl.

Compartmentalized designs, such as the herb knot or wheel, make attractive features, but they are not necessarily practical if you wish to grow a large quantity of material. If this is the case, try a simple layout of rectangular beds, separated by wide paths.

RIGHT: Large raised beds edged in timber are ideal for herbs, allowing space for the different plants to develop.

LEFT: Taller growing, woody herbs make wonderful aromatic hedges for lining pathways and dividing key areas. These include lavender; the aptly named *Rosmarinus officinalis* 'Miss Jessopp's Upright'; cotton lavender; hyssop; *Rosa rugosa* varieties, and, for a tall hedge in mild areas only, sweet bay.

BELOW: It helps to have some kind of aide-mémoire in the herb garden, so that you can identify the plants at a glance, be reminded of their use and avoid making mistakes. This is particularly important if you are growing edible and medicinal herbs together, since the latter may be poisonous. Use pieces of split slate and paint the words with a fine brush. Alternatively, use broad plant labels and write on them with pencil or a waterproof marker. Visitors will enjoy reading titbits of historical information, folklore and legend. Another approach would be to have a numbered key with the main list kept indoors.

A Lovers' Knot

Knot gardens are highly symbolic, their intertwining and never-ending patterns representing themes of endless love.

Knot gardens reached their heyday in the sixteenth century, but are now popular again. The knot is made from low hedges. Dwarf box (*Buxus sempervirens* 'Suffruticosa') has long been a popular choice —with the pattern in-filled with blocks of low-growing or carpeting herbs, such as lawn chamomile, creeping thyme, chives, golden marjoram, parsley and purple basil. An alternative is to use woody herbs, which can be clipped to form low hedges. Such an approach is often most effective if the spaces in-between are filled with gravel or stone chippings. If you do this, prepare the ground thoroughly first and then lay landscaping fabric to

suppress weeds. Mark the design on the fabric using coloured chalks. For a more unusual effect, use different coloured heging plants, clipped to look as though they pass over or under one another. The following are all suitable:

- Cotton lavender (*Santolina chamaecyparissus*)
- Dwarf lavender (e.g. *Lavandula angustifolia* 'Munstead' or 'Hidcote')
- Hyssop (*Hyssopus officinalis*)
- Shrubby thymes (e.g. *Thymus vulgaris* 'Silver Posie'; *T.* x *citriodorus* varieties)
- Wall germander (*Teucrium chamaedrys*)

ABOVE: Herb gardens traditionally have a central focus, such as a stone sundial, or a topiary feature, like a sweet bay standard. For larger gardens you might consider a circular seat, a formal raised pool or a rose-covered gazebo.

Kitchen Herbs

There is nothing to compare with the flavour of fresh herbs, and one of the great delights of having a garden is that you are able to grow your own instead of relying on what the supermarket has to offer.

S OME CULINARY herbs, such as basil, chervil, coriander (cilantro) and summer savory, are annuals or tender perennials and have to be replaced each year; if you don't have the facilities to grow your own, you can usually obtain new plants from the garden centre. Many other culinary herbs are perennial and go on producing year after year, given appropriate care.

It may seem obvious, but herbs for cooking need to be within easy reach of the kitchen. You're unlikely to want to tramp halfway across the garden in the rain to collect ingredients for a bouquet garni, so you'll appreciate having a small collection of key culinary herbs in containers near the door. You can also pot up a few perennial herbs for winter supplies on the kitchen windowsill, or bring potted herbs into the greenhouse or conservatory to keep them cropping. To develop the most intense flavour outdoor cultivation is usually necessary.

LEFT: Some kitchen herbs dry particularly well, especially the woody ones, such as sage, tarragon, savory, rosemary, thyme and bay. Tie small sprigs together and dry bunches upside down in a warm airy place out of direct sunlight. To package them once dry, pick off individual leaves, keeping them whole if possible. Store in dark airtight glass jars to preserve their flavour.

FAR LEFT: Use fresh herbs to flavour extra virgin olive oil for cooking. Push sprigs of woody herbs like thyme, tarragon and rosemary into the bottle, with whole mixed peppercorns and a chilli pepper.

Potted Herbs

Most culinary herbs thrive in porous terracotta, and pot cultivation is ideal if you garden on heavy, poorly drained clay. Raise pots on 'feet' to ensure good drainage. Grow moisture-loving herbs, such as mints, in glazed pots and keep them well watered and out of strong sunlight. Top-dress herb pots with fish, blood and bone fertilizer in spring.

The best herbs for flavour are usually the straight species, rather than the coloured leaf or variegated varieties. Make sure that you grow sufficient quantities of your favourites, perhaps planting these as edgings. If you like Italian cooking, for example, you'll probably need plenty of basil and oregano; if you prefer spicy Asian foods, you'll need coriander (cilantro) in quantity. Crop herbs regularly to keep a succession of fresh, young, tasty shoots and don't allow the plants to mature and flower unless they are grown for their seeds, as this has an adverse effect on flavour. Some herbs, particularly the thymes and other labiates, taste better when grown 'hard' in full sun on sharply drained, poorish soil. Others, such as mint, need plenty of moisture to avoid mildew.

KEY

D = likes sharp drainage

E = evergreen

FH = one of the *fines herbes*

M = likes plentiful moisture

R = likes rich soil

S = likes full sun

Sh = prefers or tolerates some shade

W = well drained, but moisture retentive soil

ABOVE: Fresh blooms can be used for garnishing savoury dishes, decorating desserts, adding to salads and cooling summer drinks. Try nasturtium, mint, lavender, viola, primrose, chives, pot marigold, borage, rose petals, sweet rocket or clove pink for colourful and edible additions.

- Basil (*Ocimum basilicum*) purple basil is particularly well flavoured W S
- Bay (*Laurus nobilis*) W R S E
- Chervil (*Anthriscus cerefolium*) W S (FH)
- Chives (*Allium schoenoprasum*) W R S/Sh
- Coriander (*Coriandrum sativum*) D R S
- Dill (*Anethum graveolens*) self-seeds readily and crosses with fennel, so keep the two separate D R S
- Fennel leaf (*Foeniculum vulgare*) grow separately from dill and coriander to prevent crossing W S
- Lemon balm (*Melissa officinalis*) M S
- Lovage (*Levisticum officinale*) W R S/Sh
- Mint (*Mentha*) try applemint (*M. suaveolens*), Bowles' mint (*M. x villosa* var. *alopecuroides*) and eau de cologne mint (*M. piperita* f. *citrata*) M R S/Sh

- Oregano (*Origanum vulgare*) D R S
- Parsley – French or flat leaf (*Petroselinum crispum*) M R S/Sh (FH)
- Rosemary (*Rosmarinus officinalis*) D E S
- Sage (*Salvia officinalis*) D E S
- Sorrel (*Rumex acetosa*) M R S/Sh
- Summer savory (*Satureja hortensis*) W R S
- Sweet cicely (*Myrrhis odorata*) M Sh
- Sweet marjoram (*Origanum majorana*) D S R
- Tarragon (French, *Artemisia dracunculus*) D E R (FH)
- Thyme (common, *Thymus vulgaris*) or the stronger flavoured broad-leaf thyme, *T. pulegiodes*) D E S
- Winter savory (*Satureja montana*) D E S

Note: Many herbs prefer alkaline soil.

Decorative Flowers & Herbs

Many of the traditional perennials of the flower border are actually ancient herbs that were originally cultivated because of their medicinal properties or because they were attractive to bees.

OUR MODERN-DAY understanding of what constitutes a herb is significantly different to that of the past. Nowadays, we think of a narrow group of shrubs with aromatic properties, but in days gone by many flowers were thought to have a practical application in the home or medicine chest. Herbs tend to be survivors. As their long cultivation history suggests, they are easily propagated, mostly self-supporting and disease-free. Such was the value placed on herbs that over the centuries an astounding number of different cultivars and varieties have survived. Even today, experts occasionally rediscover a flower believed lost to cultivation, growing in an old cottage garden.

Herbs with small leaves or diaphanous flowers such as lady's mantle (*Alchemilla mollis*) may be used to provide a soft infill or backdrop for flowering shrubs, perennials or bulbs that have large, well-structured blooms. Examples include feathery bronze fennel as a foil for red or orange dahlias; sweet rocket (*Hesperis matronalis*) among Russell hybrid lupins; and white-flowered musk mallow (*Malva moschata* 'Alba'), with its deeply divided leaves, as an accompaniment to roses.

Flowering herbs come in all shapes and sizes, so it is easy to put together a pleasing arrangement with contrasting forms and textures. There are bold blooms, such as the Madonna lily, peony and opium poppy, and stately spires or architectural specimens for use as dramatic accent plants. Although tall, bulky herbs, such as Joe Pye weed, tansy, valerian and elecampane, are best at the back of a border, plants with a slender or sculptural profile work well towards the front. It is much more interesting visually to modulate the heights of plants, and this occurs naturally with self-seeders such as granny's bonnets (*Aquilegia*) and mullein (*Verbascum*).

LEFT: Small parterres with intricate patterns, such as this one made from clipped English or dwarf box (*Buxus sempervirens* 'Suffruticosa') can be planted with compact ornamental herbs including chives, variegated thymes, golden marjoram, purple basil and dwarf lavenders.

Accent Plants

Herbs with tall, slender flower spikes or an architectural profile make eye-catching focal points. Choose from the following:

- Angelica (*Angelica archangelica*) B
- Clary sage (*Salvia sclarea* var. *sclarea*) B
- Cotton or Scotch thistle (*Onopordum acanthium*)
- Evening primrose (*Oenothera biennis*) B
- Fennel (*Foeniculum vulgare*)
- Foxglove* (*Digitalis purpurea*) B
- Madonna lily (*Lilium candidum*)
- Monkshood* (*Aconitum*)
- Mullein (*Verbascum*) B
- Viper's bugloss (*Echium vulgare*) B

B = biennial or short-lived perennial   *poisonous

Flowering Edging

Some of the low-growing herbs, such as dwarf lavender, are particularly suited to edging. Others for the cottage border include:

- Catmint (*Nepeta* x *faassenii*)
- Chives (*Allium schoenoprasum*)
- Cranesbill (*Geranium* species and cultivars e.g. 'Johnson's Blue')
- Dead nettle (*Lamium maculatum* varieties)
- Forget-me-not (*Myosotis sylvatica*) B
- Lady's mantle (*Alchemilla mollis*)
- Marjoram (*Origanum* species and cultivars)
- Clove pink (*Dianthus* species)

Variegated & Coloured Leaf Herbs

These herbs add splashes of colour in the flower border or in container plantings. Use them to enhance the colours of a flower-filled summer pot, or plant them in the garden to add interest to areas without flowers.

PURPLE:

- Bronze fennel (*Foeniculum vulgare* 'Purpureum')
- Purple basil (*Ocimum basilicum*, e.g. 'Dark Opal', 'Purple Ruffles')
- Purple orach (*Atriplex hortensis* var. *rubra*)
- Purple sage (*Salvia officinalis* 'Purpurascens')

YELLOW:

- Ginger mint (*Mentha* x *gracilis* 'Variegata')
- Golden feverfew (*Tanacetum parthenium* 'Aureum')
- Variegated lemon balm (*Melissa officinalis* 'Aurea')
- Variegated sage (*Salvia officinalis* 'Icterina')

SILVER & GREY:

- Cotton lavender (*Santolina chamaecyparissus*)
- Curry plant (*Helichrysum italicum*)
- Lavender (*Lavandula* species and cultivars)
- Rue* (*Ruta graveolens* 'Jackman's Blue') *Sap may cause severe skin blistering. Do not plant in a garden used by children.
- Wormwood (*Artemisia absinthium*, e.g. 'Lambrook Silver')

WHITE:

- Variegated apple mint (*Mentha suaveolens* 'Variegata')
- Variegated nasturtium (*Tropaeolum* Alaska series)

Aromatic Sensations

Most herbs release their aromatic oils at the slightest touch. In the garden, perfume adds a magical dimension, and herbs and fragrant flowers can transform the atmosphere of a sunny patio or terrace.

TRY PUTTING POTS of your favourites near seats. Sweet basil is irresistible, and plants such as rosemary, mint and lemon-scented thyme are also likely to be touched repeatedly. Another group of aromatic herbs are the scented-leaf geraniums. The bushy *Pelargonium* 'Graveolens' releases a powerful lemon fragrance whenever the leaves are disturbed. Others in the group smell of lime, orange or rose. If you have room on a warm wall, you might also consider planting the tender shrub, lemon verbena (*Aloysia triphylla*). Its citrus aroma is heavenly. Reaching over 1.5m/5ft in some situations, it thrives in poor, well-drained soils. A winter mulch of straw protects the roots.

LEFT: Seats made from turf or planted with aromatic herbs were popular in medieval times. Many of the large gardens were enclosed by a bank, just the right height for a seat. You can make a similar feature by planting a raised bed or retaining wall. The following plants are ideal, as they withstand some wear and need only occasional clipping: chamomile (non-flowering *Chamaemelum nobile* 'Treneague'), creeping pennyroyal (*Mentha pulegium*) and *Thymus pulegioides* 'Aureus'.

RIGHT: A sheltered environment created by walls or hedges prevents fragrance from dissipating. Humidity captures and concentrates aromatic oils, which may be why herb and rose gardens have featured pools and fountains since ancient times.

Herbs for Treading

Low-growing prostrate and creeping aromatic herbs may be planted into paving by lifting bricks and paving stones or by leaving joints without mortar. Alternatively, plant up a chequerboard design of paving and herbs. Ideal herbs for this include:

- Thyme (many species and varieties, including forms of *Thymus serpyllum* and woolly thyme, *T. pseudolanuginosus*)
- Lawn chamomile (*Chamaemelum nobile* 'Treneague')
- Corsican mint (*Mentha requienii*) – best in shade with some moisture
- Creeping pennyroyal (*Mentha pulegium*)
- Corn mint (*Mentha arvensis*)
- Golden marjoram (*Origanum vulgare* 'Aureum')

Herb Lawns

In small courtyard gardens or places where mower access is restricted, lawns may be impractical. Instead, try creating a tranquil green space using a carpet-forming herb like lawn chamomile 'Treneague' with its fruity aroma. It is best in full sun and withstands occasional treading.

1 Weed meticulously the area to be planted and dig it over.

2 Incorporate sharp sand and horticultural grit to improve drainage. Rake the surface level.

3 Plant pot-grown, rooted cuttings at 10cm/4in intervals and water in.

4 Maintain by clipping over occasionally with hand shears and keep weed-free.

ABOVE: Some herbs release their oils in quantity when the foliage is disturbed. Make use of this fact by lining a walkway with them. One of the most delightful is rosemary. Planted as a hedge, the erect-growing 'Miss Jessopp's Upright' would create an aromatic wall to brush against. Old English lavender (*Lavandula angustifolia*) is perfect for lining a narrow path in a hot sunny spot, since the heat will also help to release its fragrant oils. Meanwhile, in a semi-wild garden, try more unruly herbs that encroach over the pathway, such as lemon balm and mints. Lovage and bronze fennel also work well.

Index

Acknowledgements

Anness Publishing Ltd would like to thank the following
photographers for the images in this book:

Peter Anderson, Jonathan Buckley, Marie O'Hara, Jacqui Hurst,
Andrea Jones, Simon McBride, Peter McHoy, Debbie Patterson,
Steven Wooster, Polly Wreford.

Thanks to The Garden Picture Library for permission to print the
image on p62 top, to Jenny Hendy for the images on p19 top left,
p35 top right, p60 bottom.

Clare Hall made and designed the wire chicken on p64, and Mary
Rawlinson designed the seat beneath the tree on p30.